NEW WEATH

PAUL MULDOON
New Weather

faber

First published in 1973
by Faber & Faber Ltd
The Bindery
51 Hatton Garden
London, ECIN 8HN
This edition first published in 2023

Typeset by Typo•glyphix, Burton-on-Trent
Printed in the UK by TJ Books Ltd, Padstow, Cornwall

A CIP record for this book is available from the British Library

ISBN 978-0-571-38442-6

Printed and bound in the UK on FSC® certified paper in line with our continuing
commitment to ethical business practices, sustainability and the environment.
For further information see faber.co.uk/environmental-policy

2 4 6 8 10 9 7 5 3 1

for my Fathers and Mothers

Acknowledgements

Acknowledgements are due to the editors of: *An Anthology of Irish Poetry* (Talbot), *Aquarius*, *The Faber Book of Irish Verse*, *The Honest Ulsterman*, *The Listener*, *New Irish Writing*, *The Newman Review*, *New Poems from Ulster*, *The New Statesman*, *P.E.N. New Poems* 1971–72 (Hutchinson), *Phoenix*, *Poetry Introduction* 2 (Faber), *The Sphere Book of Modern Irish Poetry*, *The Tablet*, *Threshold*, *Times Literary Supplement*; also to the Arts Council of Northern Ireland and the BBC (Radio 3, and Radio 4).

Contents

Introduction

On 30 September 1970, Seamus Heaney wrote to me from Berkeley, California:

> From our window we can just make out the faint hump of Alcatraz behind the dreamy silhouette of the Golden Gate. I haven't been into San Francisco yet but when we get a car and get more settled, we'll make it. And I'll send you a poster I took off a board here (the town is a free for all bill-board among other things) about Alcatraz. I think your poem on that theme is unforgettable.

The poem to which Seamus Heaney was referring is 'The Indians on Alcatraz', a musing on such parallels as might be found between the 1969–71 occupation by Native American activists of the former prison in San Francisco Bay and the political activism now every day evident in Northern Ireland. The last poem in *New Weather*, 'The Year of the Sloes', picked up on this theme and was written in direct response to the killing in Derry of 13 civilians by members of the Parachute Regiment. I started the poem almost immediately after Bloody Sunday, which happened on 30 January 1972, and wrote it in a frenzy. The poem drew substantially on the Native American milieu so memorably presented by Dee Brown in *Bury My Heart at Wounded Knee: An Indian History of the American West*, a book I'd read immediately upon its publication in 1970. The final image of the poem, with its representation of Native Americans being 'persuaded to lie still, / One beside the other / Right across the Great Plains', refers in its essence to that heart-stopping passage in Thoreau's *Walden*:

We do not ride on the railroad; it rides upon us. Did you ever think what those sleepers are that underlie the railroad? Each one is a man, an Irishman, or a Yankee man. The rails are laid on them, and they are covered with sand, and the cars run smoothly over them. They are sound sleepers, I assure you. And every few years a new lot is laid down and run over; so that, if some have the pleasure of riding on a rail, others have the misfortune to be ridden upon.

The dedicatee of 'The Year of the Sloes' is Ishi, the last member of the Californian Yahi tribe who had been found in 1911 and spent the five remaining years of his life on exhibit in the Museum of Anthropology in San Francisco, patiently and painstakingly making arrowheads out of shards of glass. The name 'Ishi' means 'person' in the Yahi language, though at the heart of the name are the initials of the aforementioned Seamus Heaney, who had been such a champion of my work from so early on and to whom I owed such a great debt. I had first met him in 1968, when I was sixteen years old. He shortly after published me in *Threshold*, the magazine of the Lyric Theatre, Belfast. He steered me in the direction of Karl Miller, literary editor of *The Listener*, who also published my early poems. Moreover, he put me in touch with Charles Monteith, our fellow Ulsterman, who was Poetry Editor at Faber and Faber. I was included in Faber's *Poetry Introduction 2*, which came out in 1972. As it happens, it was on 9 April 1972 that Seamus Heaney wrote to our joint editor, Charles Monteith, as follows:

> Also, I agree with you about changing Paul's title. *New Weather* has got that open ring of possibility about it.

Needless to say, I wasn't privy at the time to this behind-the-scenes conversation. My original title for the collection was *The*

Electric Orchard, after a poem that referred specifically to the apple-growing district of North Armagh in which I was brought up. Seamus Heaney's phrase about a 'ring of possibility' is reminiscent of a line from 'Linen Town', set on High Street, Belfast, in 1786:

> Smell the tidal Lagan:
> Take a last turn with citizens
> In the *tang of possibility*.

'Linen Town' was included in *Wintering Out*, Seamus Heaney's 1972 collection. There seems to be a connection, conscious or otherwise, between the idea of the privation of the winter season and the possibilities of spring associated with 'new weather.'

My own view is that, had he realized he might be introducing an element of competition between myself and him, Seamus Heaney would not have so readily agreed with Monteith's suggestion. It does seem, mind you, that Monteith wasn't at all sure how to pitch this book other than *against* something. The fact that the first edition of *New Weather* was set entirely in italics rather than roman type would suggest that there was a more than faint air of desperation as to how to signal just how 'other' these poems might be. If, indeed, it was an entirely deliberate decision. At the time, Charles Monteith had written to me to say that the printer had mistakenly set the four sample pages of the book in italics. He rather liked how they looked. What did I think? I'm pretty sure that had Monteith suggested we print in book in capitals, upside down, I would have gone along with it. The question which I've never been able to satisfactorily answer is whether a printer would indeed have taken it upon itself to make such a decision, or offer such a suggestion.

Reading *New Weather* with the dubious advantage of hindsight, I'm struck less by how 'other' it looks than by its fairly obvious influences. I'm thinking of the English poets – Larkin, Hughes, and Gunn – who were so to the fore at the time and whom I'd studied extensively at school. The outlandish metaphor-making, as in 'Hedgehog' or 'The Goldfish', may be laid at the door of John Donne. A number of reviewers of *New Weather* commented on its indebtedness to Robert Frost, a poet whose 'Tree at My Window' with its 'Your head so much concerned with outer, / mine with inner, weather' informs 'Wind and Tree' even more that I realized at the time. The other, less evident, influence on that poem is an Irish triad:

> *dhá dtrian gréine fá bheannaibh,*
> *dhá dtrian gaoithe fá chrannaibh,*
> *dhá dtrian galair le hoíche*

> (two-thirds of sunlight happens around mountains,
> two-thirds of wind happens around trees,
> two-thirds of illness happens at night).

To which one might add, 'two-thirds of a poet's obsessions may be found in a first collection'.

PAUL MULDOON
New York, 2023

NEW WEATHER

The Electric Orchard

The early electric people had domesticated the wild ass.
They knew all about falling off.
Occasionally, they would have fallen out of the trees.
Climbing again, they had something to prove
To their neighbours. And they did have neighbours.
The electric people lived in villages
Out of their need of security and their constant hunger.
Together they would divert their energies

To neutral places. Anger to the banging door,
Passion to the kiss.
And electricity to earth. Having stolen his thunder
From an angry god, through the trees
They had learned to string his lightning.
The women gathered random sparks into their aprons,
A child discovered the swing
Among the electric poles. Taking everything as given,

The electric people were confident, hardly proud.
They kept fire in a bucket,
Boiled water and dry leaves in a kettle, watched the lid
By the blue steam lifted and lifted.
So that, where one of the electric people happened to fall,
It was accepted as an occupational hazard.
There was something necessary about the thing. The North Wall
Of the Eiger was notorious for blizzards,

If one fell there his neighbour might remark, Bloody fool.
All that would have been inappropriate,
Applied to the experienced climber of electric poles.
I have achieved this great height?
No electric person could have been that proud,
Thirty or forty feet. Perhaps not that,
If the fall happened to be broken by the roof of a shed.
The belt would burst, the call be made,

The ambulance arrive and carry the faller away
To hospital with a scream.
There and then the electric people might invent the railway,
Just watching the lid lifted by the steam.
Or decide that all laws should be based on that of gravity,
Just thinking of the faller fallen.
Even then they were running out of things to do and see.
Gradually, they introduced legislation

Whereby they nailed a plaque to every last electric pole.
They would prosecute any trespassers.
The high up, singing and live fruit liable to shock or kill
Were forbidden. Deciding that their neighbours
And their neighbours' innocent children ought to be stopped
For their own good, they threw a fence
Of barbed wire round the electric poles. None could describe
Electrocution, falling, the age of innocence.

Wind and Tree

In the way that the most of the wind
Happens where there are trees,

Most of the world is centred
About ourselves.

Often where the wind has gathered
The trees together and together,

One tree will take
Another in her arms and hold.

Their branches that are grinding
Madly together and together,

It is no real fire.
They are breaking each other.

Often I think I should be like
The single tree, going nowhere,

Since my own arm could not and would not
Break the other. Yet by my broken bones

I tell new weather.

Blowing Eggs

This is not the nest
That has been pulling itself together
In the hedge's intestine.
It is the cup of a boy's hands,

Whereby something is lost
More than the necessary heat gone forever
And death only after beginning.
There is more to this pale blue flint

In this careful fist
Than a bird's nest having been discovered
And a bird not sitting again.
This is the start of the underhand,

The way that he has crossed
These four or five delicate fields of clover
To hunker by this crooked railing.
This is the breathless and the intent

Puncturing of the waste
And isolate egg and this the clean delivery
Of little yolk and albumen.
These his wrists, surprised and stained.

Thrush

I guessed the letter
    Must be yours. I recognized
The cuttle ink,
    The serif on
The P. I read the postmark and the date,
    Impatience held
By a paperweight.
    I took your letter at eleven
To the garden
    With my tea.
And suddenly the yellow gum secreted
    Halfwayup
The damson bush
    Had grown a shell.
I let those scentless pages fall
    And took it
In my feckless hand. I turned it over
    On its back
To watch your mouth
    Withdraw. Making a lean, white fist
Out of my freckled hand.

The Glad Eye

Bored by Ascham and Zeno
In private conversation on the longbow,

I went out onto the lawn.
Taking the crooked bow of yellow cane,

I shot an arrow over
The house and wounded my brother.

He cried those huge dark tears
Till they had blackened half his hair.

Zeno could have had no real
Notion of the flying arrow being still,

Not blessed with the hindsight
Of photography and the suddenly frozen shot,

Yet that obstinate one
Eye inveigled me to a standing stone.

Evil eyes have always burned
Corn black and people have never churned

Again after their blink.
That eye was deeper than the Lake of the Young,

Outstared the sun in the sky.
Could look without commitment into another eye

Hedges in Winter

Every year they have driven stake after stake after stake
Deeper into the cold heart of the hill.
Their arrowheads are more deadly than snowflakes,
Their spearheads sharper than icicles,

Yet stilled by snowflake, icicle.
They are already broken by their need of wintering,
These archers taller than any snowfall
Having to admit their broken shafts and broken strings,

Whittling the dead branches to the girls they like.
That they have hearts is visible,
The nests of birds, these obvious concentrations of black.
Yet where the soldiers will later put on mail,

The archers their soft green, nothing will tell
Of the heart of the mailed soldier seeing the spear he flung,
Of the green archer seeing his shaft kill.
Only his deliberate hand, a bird pretending a broken wing.

Macha

Macha, the Ice Age
Held you down,
Heavy as a man.
As he dragged

Himself away,
You sprang up
Big as half a county,
Curvaceous,

Drumlin country.
Now at war
With men,
Leading them against

Each other,
You had to prove
Your permanence.
You scored the ground

With a sharp brooch,
Mapped your first
Hillfort.
The day you fell,

At the hands of men,
You fell
Back over half a county.
Clutching a town

To your breasts.

The Waking Father

My father and I are catching spricklies
Out of the Oona river.
They have us feeling righteous,
The way we have thrown them back.
Our benevolence is astounding.

When my father stood out in the shallows
It occurred to me that
The spricklies might have been piranhas,
The river a red carpet
Rolling out from where he had just stood,

Or I wonder now if he is dead or sleeping.
For if he is dead I would have his grave
Secret and safe,
I would turn the river out of its course,
Lay him in its bed, bring it round again.

              No one would question
That he had treasures or his being a king,
Telling now of the real fish farther down.

Dancers at the Moy

This Italian square
And circling plain
Black once with mares
And their stallions,
The flat Blackwater
Turning its stones

Over hour after hour
As their hooves shone
And lifted together
Under the black rain,
One or other Greek war
Now coloured the town

Blacker than ever before
With hungry stallions
And their hungry mares
Like hammocks of skin,
The flat Blackwater
Unable to contain

Itself as horses poured
Over acres of grain
In a black and gold river.
No band of Athenians
Arrived at the Moy fair
To buy for their campaign,

Peace having been declared
And a treaty signed.
The black and gold river
Ended as a trickle of brown
Where those horses tore
At briars and whins,

Ate the flesh of each other
Like people in famine.
The flat Blackwater
Hobbled on its stones
With a wild stagger
And sag in its backbone,

The local people gathered
Up the white skeletons.
Horses buried for years
Under the foundations
Give their earthen floors
The ease of trampolines.

Identities

When I reached the sea
I fell in with another who had just come
From the interior. Her family
Had figured in a past regime
But her father was now imprisoned.

She had travelled, only by night,
Escaping just as her own warrant
Arrived and stealing the police boat,
As far as this determined coast.

As it happened, we were staying at the same
Hotel, pink and goodish for the tourist
Quarter. She came that evening to my room
Asking me to go to the capital,
Offering me wristwatch and wallet,
To search out an old friend who would steal
Papers for herself and me. Then to be married,
We could leave from that very harbour.

I have been wandering since, back up the streams
That had once flowed simply one into the other,
One taking the other's name.

Clonfeacle

It happened not far away
In this meadowland
That Patrick lost a tooth.
I translate the placename

As we walk along
The river where he washed,
That translates stone to silt.
The river would preach

As well as Patrick did.
A tongue of water passing
Between teeth of stones.
Making itself clear,

Living by what it says,
Converting meadowland to marsh.
You turn towards me,
Coming round to my way

Of thinking, holding
Your tongue between your teeth.
I turn my back on the river
And Patrick, their sermons

Ending in the air.

February

He heard that in Derryscollop there is a tree
For every day of the year,
And the extra tree is believed to grow
One year in every four.

He had never yet taken time to grieve
For this one without breasts
Or that one wearing her heart on her sleeve
Or another with her belly slashed.

He had never yet taken time to love
The blind pink fledgeling fallen out of the nest
Of one sleeping with open mouth
And her head at a list.

What was he watching and waiting for,
Walking Scollop every day?
For one intending to leave at the end of the year,
Who would break the laws of time and stay.

Kate Whiskey

I kept the whiskey in the caves
Well up in the hills. It was never safe
To have it about the houses,
Always crawling with excise and police.

The people could still get the stuff
As often as they liked, and easily enough,
For those were still the days
When making whiskey broke nobody's laws.

Selling it, though, was as grave
An offence as teaching those people to love,
Fathers and husbands and boys.

Water rushed through my caves with a noise
To tell me how I should always live.
I sold the water, the whiskey I would give.

Thinking of the Goldfish

Replacing the lid of air
On its circle of water,
Thinking of the goldfish was

My classic final gesture.
Beating in its plastic bag,
It looked like a change of heart

I had bought for you to hold.
It was far too cold, so cold
There was nothing I could do

But leave it behind to die
At the top of the old house,
Its head in the clouds

Of its own breath. So I locked
The door, took your hand and word
And followed you. Only glad

Of the law that I would always
Own the light above my head,
If simply borrow from my side.

Vespers

It looks like there's
Nothing for it
But the bare floor.
You've given one blanket
Off the single bed

By way of reasonableness.
Couldn't we go to sleep
Together for once,
If only of necessity?
We could always keep

The sheet between us.
I'll do nothing you won't.
We'll both be colder
For being lost in thought,
Setting up difficulties

Where none ought to exist.
I'll put out the light,
And the night has fallen
Bodily and silent
Through the defunct window.

The frost has designs on it.

The Cure for Warts

Had I been the seventh son of a seventh son
Living at the dead centre of a wood
Or at the dead end of a lane,
I might have cured by my touch alone
That pair of warts nippling your throat,

Who had no faith in a snail rubbed on your skin
And spiked on a thorn like a king's head,
In my spittle on shrunken stone,
In bathing yourself at the break of dawn
In dew or the black cock's or the bull's blood,

In other such secrets told by way of a sign
Of the existence of one or other god,
So I doubt if any woman's son
Could have cured by his touch alone
That pair of warts nibbling your throat.

Leaving an Island

The woman of the house
Is letting out the chickens.
Air trapped in the capsized

Boat where they coop
Is visible to the naked eye.
I see through you

In your crocheted dress.
Elevenses. Woman of the house,
This is just to say

We have left no clues.
Ferdinand, Miranda,
It was pure and simple.

Thank you, thank you.
For the dulse. For everything.
I read between your legs

And recognize that you who took
The world into your mouth
Have taught me ships in bottles,

The sea in shells,

The Radio Horse

I believed in those plains
Without grass or sky,
A levelled silence
Broken only by the credible woods.
Then the first soft thud
Of a horse by radio,

And already I could sense
This horse would carry
Not only the plans
Of that one's plot or counterplot
But your realer secrets.
Your intending to go

In your own hand or evidence
To prove you another spy
Infiltrating my lines.
If only you were as easily waylaid,
Predictable in your road,
As a horse by radio,

Its tittering in one distance
That clatters, thunders by,
Then thins and thins.
I believed in your riding all night
Lathered by your own sweat,
Your dressing as boys

Keeping in their shirts or jeans
Messages for my eyes only,
Whose latest are canc-
Elled to a word, that lost in codes,
Telling of their being delayed
By horses' thrown shoes.

Good Friday, 1971. Driving Westward

It was good going along with the sun
Through Ballygawley, Omagh and Strabane.
I started out as it was getting light
And caught sight of hares all along the road
That looked to have been taking a last fling,
Doves making the most of their offerings
As if all might not be right with the day

Where I moved through morning towards the sea.
I was glad that I would not be alone.
Those children who travel badly as wine
Waved as they passed in their uppity cars
And now the first cows were leaving the byres,
The first lorry had delivered its load.
A whole country was fresh after the night

Though people were still fighting for the last
Dreams and changing their faces where
I paused To read the first edition of the truth.
I gave a lift to the girl out of love
And crossed the last great frontier at Lifford.
Marooned by an iffing and butting herd
Of sheep, Letterkenny had just then laid

Open its heart and we passed as new blood
Back into the grey flesh of Donegal.
The sky went out of its way for the hills
And life was changing down for the sharp bends
Where the road had put its thin brown arm round
A hill and held on tight out of pure fear.
Errigal stepped out suddenly in our

Path and the thin arm tightened round the waist
Of the mountain and for a time I lost
Control and she thought we hit something big
But I had seen nothing, perhaps a stick
Lying across the road. I glanced back once
And there was nothing but a heap of stones.
We had just dropped in from nowhere for lunch

In Gaoth Dobhair, I happy and she convinced
Of the death of more than lamb or herring.
She stood up there and then, face full of drink,
And announced that she and I were to blame
For something killed along the way we came.
Children were warned that it was rude to stare,
Left with their parents for a breath of air.

Seanchas

Coming here, we were like that mountain whose base
We kept sidestepping. Thinking ourselves superior.
Having, we thought, our final attitude and bias.
Really, wanting a new slant. For the past hour
We heard the seanchai relearn
What he has always known,

Region of heroes, gentle maidens,
Giants that war and landgrab.
Each phrase opening like a fern.
Till some make fists of themselves, like the stones
In a landslide, a cadence
That comes in his way. He can adlib
No other route. If we play back the tape
He may take up where he left off.

Nothing. And no heroes people this landscape
Through which he sees us off.
The lifted wondering faces of his sheep
Stare back at us like nimble rain clouds, their bellies
Accumulate and are anonymous again. But having shape,
Separate and memorable.

Behold the Lamb

You were first.
The ewe licked clean ochre and lake
But you would not move.
Weighted with stones yet
Dead your dead head floats.
Better dead than sheep,

The thin worm slurred in your gut,
The rot in your feet,
The red dog creeping at dawn.
Better than dipped in the hard white water,
Your stomach furred,
Your head hardboiled.

Better dead than dyed
In a bowl of pale whin petals.
Better than rolling down the hill,
Pale skull flaking.
First to break.
First for the scream of the clean bite.

Better dead with your delph head floating.

Hedgehog

The snail moves like a
Hovercraft, held up by a
Rubber cushion of itself,
Sharing its secret

With the hedgehog. The hedgehog
Shares its secret with no one.
We say, Hedgehog, come out
Of yourself and we will love you.

We mean no harm. We want
Only to listen to what
You have to say. We want
Your answers to our questions.

The hedgehog gives nothing
Away, keeping itself to itself.
We wonder what a hedgehog
Has to hide, why it so distrusts.

We forget the god
Under this crown of thorns.
We forget that never again
Will a god trust in the world.

Lives of the Saints

Others have sought publicity
But the saints looked for higher things.
The people getting ready to fly
Off the roofs of public buildings
Had their eyes on the actual sky,
Never spreading their linen or bamboo wings

So briefly for a public death
Had they really been saints of the old school.
Those saints have the last laugh
At the reporters for the Chronicles
And the people taking photographs.
I think especially of Brendan setting sail

One day the sea was blueblack
As his body that overnight he had beaten,
Drifting along wherever God liked
And the people living by bread alone
Shouting after Good Luck, Good Luck.
All the Chronicles agreed. The boat was stone.

Easter Island

Stonehenge, Newgrange,
Were engineered

By men who whinged
In slow motion.

Thinking in terms
Of a stone's throw,

They crept with sickles
To steal a kiss

Under the mistletoe.
These islanders

Might winch for miles
To right abstractions

From the living rock.
No resurrection but

The Moving Stone
Compelled their homage.

The Indians on Alcatraz

Through time their sharp features
Have softened and blurred,
As if they still inhabited
The middle distances,
As if these people have never
Stopped riding hard

In an opposite direction,
The people of the shattered lances
Who have seemed forever going back.
To have willed this reservation,
It is as if they are decided
To be islanders at heart,

As if this island
Has forever been the destination
Of all those dwindling bands.
After the newspaper and TV reports
I want to be glad that
Young Man Afraid Of His Horses lives

As a brilliant guerrilla fighter,
The weight of his torque
Worn like the moon's last quarter,
Though only if he believes
As I believed of his fathers,
That they would not attack after dark.

Vampire

Seeing the birds in winter
Drinking the images of themselves
Reflected in a sheet of ice,
She thinks of that winter –
'Carefully appointed mirrors
Create the illusion of depth' –
When she covered her walls
From floor to ceiling with glass.

In January she would have
The 'carefully appointed mirrors'
Taken away. The thing ought
Not be bigger than the fact,
She would keep telling herself.
Or, already spending the daylight
Hours in bed, say, I am alive
Because I am alive.

For even then she believed herself
Native soil enough for herself,
Though already she would rise
Only as night was falling, quietly
Lifting the single milkbottle
That had stood on her step since morning,
The top repeatedly
Punctured by a thirsting bird.

Elizabeth

The birds begin as an isolated shower
Over the next county, their slow waltz
Swerving as if to avoid something
Every so often, getting thin
As it slants, making straight for
Us over your father's darkening fields,
Till their barely visible wings
Remember themselves, they are climbing again.
We wonder what could bring them this far

Inland, they belong to the sea.
You hold on hard like holding on to life,
Following the flock as it bends
And collapses like a breeze.
You want to know where from and why,
But birds would never keep still long enough
For me to be able to take a count.
We'll hold our ground and they'll pass.
But they're coming right overhead, you cry,

And storm inside and bang the door.
All I can hear is the flicking of bolts.
The one dull window is shutting
Its eye as if a wayward hurricane
With the name of a girl and the roar
Of devils were beginning its assaults.
But these are the birds of a child's painting,
Filling the page till nothing else is seen.
You are inside yet, pacing the floor,

Having been trapped in every way.
You hold yourself as your own captive.
My promised children are in your hands,
Hostaged by you in your father's old house.
I call you now for all the names of the day,
Lizzie and Liz and plain Beth.
You do not make the slightest sound.
When you decide that you have nothing to lose
And come out, there is nothing you can say;

We watch them hurtle, a recklessness of stars,
Into the acre that has not cooled
From my daylong ploughings and harrowings,
Their greys flecking the brown,
Till one, and then two, and now four
Sway back across your father's patchwork quilt,
Into your favourite elm. They will stay long
Enough to underline how soon they will be gone,
As you seem thinner than you were before.

The Kissing Seat

The organized crime
Of the kissing seat,
How well it holds us.
We're caught and fixed

In its ornamental S.
Oughtn't we to be here
And now?
I watch the sunset,

You the moonrise,
It's two winds blowing
At one and the same.
We're both going where

We're looking. Elsewhere.
It's getting late now,
You've only a linen shift
Between you and harm.

Can't we agree at least
On which star's the Pole,
The word on that flower,
What atrophies the kidney

Of the private pool?

Grass Widow

And of course I cried
As I watched him go away.
    Europe must have cried
For Europe had no more say
When America left her.

    No other woman
Came between us. It seemed that
When I would lock the gleaming
    Door against his weight,
It was the water in which

    I showered that inter-
Vened. And the water that slopped
From the system he was meant
To have lagged. I overslept
    That winter morning,

    And had cause, I say,
For crying, when I walloped
Through the flooding house and saw
    Him go. As Europe
Watched America, I watched.

    Now my dreams are filled
With reconciliations.
    Dreams I never willed,
Who have chosen the Ocean,
The Gulf Stream warming my heart.

[35]

Skeffington's Daughter

An Iron Maiden, brainchild of the Lieutenant
of the Tower under Henry the Eighth.

Not one to lose
Her head,
Her father had thought.
Now that her lover

Had left her pregnant,
He believed
That he understood
Her want.

Being his daughter,
She would have
Another chance.
No one would suffer,

It would be nothing
Like a death
In the family.
Leaving backstreet and foetus

Behind her,
She would again be taken
For that clever,
Careful virgin.

Not one to lose face.

Cuckoo Corn

The seed that goes into the ground
After the first cuckoo
Is said to grow short and light
As the beard of a boy.

Though Spring was slow this year
And the seed late,
After that Summer the corn was long
And heavy as the hair of any girl.

They claimed that she had no errand
Near the thresher,
This girl whose hair floated as if underwater
In a wind that would have cleaned corn,

Who was strangled by the flapping belt.
But she had reason,
I being her lover, she being that man's daughter,
Knowing of cuckoo corn, of seed and season.

The Upriver Incident

He thanked his parents for keeping still
And left them sleeping, deaf and blind
After their heavy meal,

Then stole away where the moon was full
And the dogs gave no sound.
He thanked the dogs for keeping still

And ran along the tops of the dark hills
That heaped like the sleeping anaconda
After its heavy meal,

To the bright square in the highest coil
That was the lady's window.
She thanked her parents for keeping still

And they ran together over a further hill
Like the lady's belly so hard and round
After its heavy meal,

Till they stood at the top of the waterfall,
Its deep pool where they drowned.
Let us thank waters for not keeping still
After their heavy meal.

The Lost Tribe

Has it been only two years
Since the river went on fire?
Last year your father's heart wob-
Bled while he was dusting crops,

Too heavy for his light plane.
Was it three years ago, then,
The year I shot the wild duck
And we took her clutch of eggs,

Carefully, to our own bed?
They hatched out under our heat,
Their first passions being earth
And water, the sky that curved

Far over the huddling barns.
We taught the fields of kept corn
Good for both bread and porridge,
And as they were then of age,

The rightness of wearing clothes.
We hooked up their rubber shoes
For that sad day they waddled
Back into their rightful wild,

The heaven of river banks.
They had learned to speak our tongue,
Knew it was all for the best.
Was that not the year you lost

Another child, the oil slick
Again bloodied our own creek,
All innocents were set free,
Your father had learned to fly?

The Field Hospital

Taking, giving back their lives
By the strength of our bare hands,
By the silence of our knives,
We answer to no grey South

Nor blue North, not self defence,
The lie of just wars, neither
Cold nor hot blood's difference
In their discharging of guns,

But that hillside of fresh graves.
Would this girl brought to our tents
From whose flesh we have removed
Shot that George, on his day off,

Will use to weight fishing lines,
Who died screaming for ether,
Yet protest our innocence?
George lit the lanterns, in danced

Those gigantic, yellow moths
That brushed right over her wounds,
Pinning themselves to our sleeves
Like medals given the brave.

Party Piece

The girl alone in the wood's
Corner had just then filled her
Glass with tomato and crushed
Ice. She wore a man's shrunk head
Slung over either shoulder,
A child's head hung at her waist.
He would have raped and killed her
Had this happened in the past,
Not yet telling wrong from right.
Since the world had grown older
He approached and introduced
Himself as something to eat,

Thinking still that wars were lost
Or won by hand to hand fights.
Though he had just then called her
Beautiful, they had just kissed,
She paused to bring back her dead
And his thin red line faltered.
That last war's end should have taught
The weakness of bright soldiers,
Those mushrooms at thigh and breast
Told of threat and counterthreat,
Yet they plunged helterskelter
Through a young wood and laid waste

A cornfield. Then this welter
Of steel and glass where they crashed
Through this heavy iron gate.
Their bodies are still smoulder-
Ing, they are like those old ghosts
Who skid past graveyards. Their heads,
Lifted clean off by the blast,
Lying here in the back seat
Like something dirty, hold our
Sadness in their eyes, who wished
For the explosion's heart, not
Pain's edge where we take shelter.

The Year of the Sloes, for Ishi

In the Moon
Of Frost in the Tepees,
There were two stars
That got free.
They yawned and stretched
To white hides,
One cutting a slit
In the wall of itself
And stepping out into the night.

In the Moon
Of the Dark Red Calf,
It had learned
To track itself
By following the dots
And dashes of its blood.
It knew the silence
Deeper
Than that of birds not singing.

In the Moon
Of the Snowblind,
The other fed the fire
At its heart
With the dream of a deer
Over its shoulder.
One water would wade through another,
Shivering,
Salmon of Knowledge leap the Fall.

In the Moon
Of the Red Grass Appearing,
He discovered her
Lying under a bush.
There were patches of yellowed
Snow and ice
Where the sun had not looked.
He helped her over the Black Hills
To the Ford of the Two Friends.

In the Moon
Of the Ponies Shedding,
He practised counting coups,
Knowing it harder
To live at the edge of the earth
Than its centre.
He caught the nondescript horse
And stepped
Down onto the prairies.

In the Moon
Of Making the Fat,
He killed his first bison.
Her quick knife ran under the skin
And offered the heart
To the sky.
They had been the horizon.
She saved what they could not eat
That first evening.

In the Moon
Of the Red Cherries,
She pledged that she would stay
So long as there would be
The Two-Legged
And the Four-Legged Ones,
Long as grass would grow and water
Flow, and the wind blow.
None of these things had forgotten.

In the Moon
Of the Black Cherries,
While he was looking for a place
To winter,
He discovered two wagons
Lying side by side
That tried to be a ring.
There were others in blue shirts
Felling trees for a square.

In the Moon
When the Calf Grows Hair,
There was a speck in the sky
Where he had left the tepee.
An eagle had started
Out of her side
And was waiting to return.
The fire was not cold,
The feet of six horses not circles.

In the Moon
Of the Season Changing,
He left the river
Swollen with rain.
He kicked sand over the fire.
He prepared his breast
By an ochre
That none would see his blood.
Any day now would be good to die.

In the Moon
Of the Leaves Falling,
I had just taken a bite out of the
Moon and pushed the plate
Of the world away.
Someone was asking for six troopers
Who had lain down
One after another
To drink a shrieking river.

In the Moon
Of the Trees Popping, two snails
Glittered over a dead Indian.
I realized that if his brothers
Could be persuaded to lie still,
One beside the other
Right across the Great Plains,
Then perhaps something of this original
Beauty would be retained.